No Gravity

TWO

A collection of poems by

Rudy Francisco

Cover Art: ArtofAndres

Ingredients

Page

4

I have a strong disrespect for authority and rules. Even gravity. Gravity sucks

- Sebastian Thrun

Simeona

My mother
wears her
wrinkles

the way
an ocean
wears a
wave.

She is the only
body of water

that refuses
to let me
drown.

Sam, Bob Marley and I

When Bob Marley
is on the radio,

my father and I
are the same age.

The stereo is loud,
but we sing louder.

This is how we
safeguard the
memory of us,

how we challenge
Alzheimer's to a
fist fight,

how we snarl
at the disease,

just to make sure
it knows

that we
will not go
quietly.

Bloom

No matter what you ask
of the daffodil,

it will still wait until
spring to bloom.

From this, I
learned

we all open up
when the time
is right.

Thank you

When I say I love you,
I mean, I'm held together
by rusty paper clips,

your absence is the wind
and loneliness has always
been good at making me
into debris,

I mean,
I'm sorry for turning
over the ocean and
expecting the fish
to be still,

I mean,
I'm a glass with too
much water and I know
it's not fair to ask you
to carry all this liquid
without spilling,

I mean, I know I'm
not easy to deal with.

I guess what I'm saying is,

thank you.

How Did You Lose Her?

I felt trapped,
but another man
looked at my prison
and called her a church.

Who would choose to be a jail
when given the option
of being a sanctuary?

After

Long after
I have given up,

my heart still
searches for you

without my
permission.

This

Of all the things I could've been, I am so glad to be this. Thank god I didn't actually become who I pretended to be; back when I had no idea who I was.

Ambition

Someday,
you will throw a penny
into a wishing well.

It'll choke
because your dreams are
too big for it to swallow.

Your ambition grows out
of its clothes,

hogs the armrest
at the movies,

takes up all the space
in the closet,

it's massive
and too large for anything
smaller than the sky.

Nemesis 1/30

Once again,
it is I versus the
automatic faucet.

My eager hands
dancing around
the spout, trying
to seduce a wash
from its neck,

while the silver deity
stares back, aloof,
unimpressed,

and still
holding the water
for ransom.

Empty 2/30

Some people will take
until you have nothing left

and then hold a grudge
against your hands
for being empty.

Filter 3/30

My future is a
blurry photograph
taken with an awful
camera.

I spend everyday
staring at it, editing,
trying to make
it perfect.

You are my
favorite filter.

Machine 4/30

I cannot fix you.
I can only show you
how I use the wrench,

how I turn the bolts,
how I put mistakes
in a belt and make
them tools,

how I look the
machine in the face,

call it unfinished,
call it beautiful
and give it
my name.

The Fall 5/30

When they place you
on a pedestal,

they won't ask if you
are scared of heights.

They'll just hoist you
into the sky,

drag you as close
to heaven as possible,

take your wings,
and video tape
the fall.

Shoreline 5/30

My father's memory
has become a
stubborn shoreline,

but each day
is a sneaky wave
that takes pieces
of our history
without asking.

Dementia is
selfish like that.

Storm 6/30

On days like this,
I give my sweaty hands
permission to become
the same river.

I press them into
each other,

say a prayer,
tape the windows

and wonder if you
are the storm
that I have been
preparing for.

Glass 7/30

Today, I'm a
courageous windshield,
taunting all of the
rocks.

My parents
are both stained
glass.

Which is to say,
I come from a
long line of
windows.

Which is to say,
I won't break easily.

I speak many languages,
but shatter is not
one of them.

How are You Still here? 8/30

I know the stumble,
the knockdown,
and the fall.

I've met the bruise,
the cut, the scrap
and the scab.

However,
I have become
friends with get up,
shake the dust,
and keep going.

The Hands 9/30

Bless the hands.
The way they bark
and growl into a fist,

the way they prefer peace,
but welcome fight.

May they hold what
I can't live without

and let go of the things
I cannot keep.

Sip 10/30

I take my compliments
the same way I take
my coffee.

I don't drink coffee.
The last time I did
it seared my entire mouth
and I couldn't taste
anything for three days.

I'm still learning how to
plant a smile into the soil
of my face and let it blossom
into a bouquet thank you.

I'm still learning how to
let endearment sit until
it's ready to be consumed,

hold it to my lips
and sip slowly.

Altar 11/30

What should I do when someone calls out
my patriarchy?

Let your mouth become an altar,
offer your voice as a sacrifice to
the god of teachable moments

and listen.

Well 12/30

On days like this,
my mouth is a garment
that I fashion into a smile,

happiness is a language
and though I'm not a
native speaker, the locals
can't hear my accent.

When people ask
how I'm doing,

I have the kind of honesty
that won't make them
uncomfortable.

I say,
I'm doing really well
and today,

I actually mean it.

Fairytale 13/30

We weren't
in love,

but we built
a fairy tale with
our bare hands.

We lived inside
the story

until the pages
stopped turning.

Weapon 14/30

This kindness also be a rifle.

I'm learning how to hold
the weapon without shaking,

spot hatred from a distance,

and shoot without missing
the target.

Notice 15/30

Isn't it amazing,
the way beautiful
things find us,

climb into our laps
without warning,

intimidate the worst
parts of our day

and only ask
that we notice them?

Argue 16/30

Let's tether ourselves
to incompatible ideas

and let them bark
at each other.

Allow disagreements to
fall from the sky,

welcome the floodwater
and dance in the rain.

Let's argue about something
and be ok when it's over.

R.I.P Prince 17/30

For the 1st time,
it is raining
in heaven.

All the drops
are purple.

Bury 18/30

It is impossible
to bury our idols
without putting a
piece of ourselves
into the casket.

As we watch the
grave lick its lips,

we often hope that
our heroes make
the ground so sick,

it has no choice,
but to give them back.

Lost 19/30

Bless the things
I've lost,

the people
that have left,

and the loneliness they
all traded places with.

It forced me to build
a home in the gravity
of their absence.

now,
I know better
how to treat
my visitors.

River 20/30

Let me fall into a river of you. I pray that
your water is generous, will forgive my
clumsy and teach me how to swim.

Lesson 21/30

The way we tore
into each other,

you would think
one of us swallowed
a golden ticket

and we both wanted
to know who was lucky.

Perhaps we labeled
this all wrong.

Maybe, instead of "Love",
we should have called it
"a lesson in survival."

Silence 22/30

I'm learning
that I don't always
have to make noise
to be seen,

that even my silence
has a spine, a rumble

and says, I'm here
in its native tongue.

Appropriation 23/30

Silly,
how often you confuse
customs for costumes,
culture for couture.

My body is not an
accessory that everyone
is allowed to borrow.

You don't get to
put on my face and
rent my experience.

I can't unzip this skin
after a long night.

None of this comes off
when the party is over.

Recipe 24/30

Gather your mistakes,
rinse them with honesty
and self reflection,

let dry until you
can see every choice
and the regret
becomes brittle,

cover the
entire surface
in forgiveness,

remind yourself
that you are human

and this too
is a gift.

Ash 25/30

I come from a long
line of men who
chose divorce papers
over apologies.

Men who loved their
kids, but not the women
they came out of.

I fear the amount of
escape I have in my blood.

Everyday will be a
practice in staying,
sitting in the mire,
being still in the flame

and saying, if this house
burns to the ground,
you will find whatever
is left of me

in the ash.

Strange 26/30

You are
a strange
kind of
beautiful.

The type of
magic that
foolish men
runaway from

and run back to
when it's too
late.

Meal 27/30

In a reoccurring
nightmare,

there is
a pack of rabid bullets
smelling one of my
old t-shirts,

hungry
and salivating
at the scent.

they find me with my
hands up, they don't
ask if I'm guilty,

they just eat
until their jaws
are tired
and wipe their
mouths clean when
the meal is over.

Seasons 28/30

I think of you and I
in seasons.

I remember the
spring of us.

The way we bloomed
under the sun, snatched a
few rays from the sky
and hid them inside
our laughter.

I remember the pollen
of your smile.

How it turned confetti
in the air and I'd shift
my palms sunny side up
to catch as much of it
as possible,

hoping I could keep
a piece of you with me
forever.

Leaving 29/30

Maybe,
I told you
I was leaving

because it was
the only way
you'd notice
my absence.

Reason 30/30

We are both hurting in places we can't reach
with our own hands and maybe this is the
only reason we are here.

Statue

Maybe, my imagination
grew tired of sitting
on the couch.

Maybe, my heart just
needed the exercise.

Maybe, I made you
from all the things
I thought I needed.

Maybe, I should've asked
if you wanted to be
a monument

before I started
building the statue.

Still

I always empathize
with the trees,

how they remain
still when the
flames arrive.

However, sometimes,
I envy the smoke.

The way it gets
to leave when
the heat comes.

Every time I see
a forest fire,
it reminds me
of us.

Me, still standing,
but rooted

in the same
place you left.

Empty Space

Instead of asking
why they left,

now I ask,
what beauty will
I create

in the space they
no longer occupy?

Perhaps

our fatal flaw
is that we attempt
to make forever

out of people
who are meant to
be temporary.

Bridges

Some say,
don't burn your bridges.

I say,
if necessary,
let the kerosene
kiss it on the lips
and watch it turn
to ash.

There's always
more than one way
to cross the water.

Perhaps,

we should love
ourselves so fiercely,

that when
others see us,

they know exactly
how it should be done.

Skin 2

When you are the only black man
in the whole neighborhood,

your skin is that one friend who
meets everyone before you do.

It wears a wife beater
and house shoes,

it knocks over the
neighbor's mailbox,

it cusses in front of the kids
and plays the music too loud,

but you actually don't do
any of those things.

It's 7 pm.
It's Wednesday
and you are just

walking home.

Confronting Hatred

How beautiful would it be
if we lived in a place

where everyone called
hatred by its full name,

tapped it on the shoulder,

looked into its eyes
without shaking

and said, "you cannot
live here anymore."

Pincushion

I have been the only person
of color in a classroom,

which is to say,

I know how it feels
to be a pincushion

in a cabinet
full of needles.

Party

Racism is the drunk guy
at the party

who tries
to fight everyone.

Nobody wants to
claim him.

America says nothing
and pretends they didn't
ride in the same car.

Justice & My Country

Loving my country
while advocating
for social justice,

feels like being
in love with 2 people

who are trying to
kill each other.

My highest ambition
is to crawl out from
under the wreckage

and laugh at all the things
that thought they could
bury me.

I write best
when I am either,
falling in love,
or falling apart.

Made in the USA
San Bernardino, CA
31 December 2018